CHINA
ACTIVITY BOOK

Written by	Linda Milliken
Edited by	Kathy Rogers
Cover Design by	Pete Brower
Page Design by	Pete Brower
Illustrated by	Barb Lorseyedi

METRIC CONVERSION CHART
Refer to this chart when metric conversions are not found within the activity.

¼ tsp	=	1.25 ml	350° F	=	175° C
½ tsp	=	2.5 ml	375° F	=	190° C
1 tsp	=	5 ml	400° F	=	200° C
1 Tbsp	=	15 ml	425° F	=	220° C
¼ cup	=	60 ml	1 inch	=	2.54 cm
⅓ cup	=	75 ml	1 foot	=	30 cm
½ cup	=	125 ml	1 yard	=	91 cm
1 cup	=	230 ml	1 mile	=	1.6 km
	1 oz.	=	28 g		
	1 lb.	=	.45 kg		

EP069 • ©1995, 2003 Edupress, Inc.™ • P.O. Box 883 • Dana Point, CA 92629
www.edupressinc.com
ISBN 1-56472-069-1
Printed in USA

TABLE OF CONTENTS

• **The Enchanted Tapestry; A Chinese Folk Tale**
by Robert D. San Souci;
Dial LB 1987. (1-3)
Gravely ill, a woman sends her sons to retrieve her tapestry, but only the youngest succeeds.

• **Yeh-Shen; A Cinderella Story From China**
by Ai-Ling Louie;
Putnam 1982. (2-6)
A Chinese story about a poor girl living with her cruel stepmother and stepsisters.

• **Journey Through China**
by Philip Steele;
Troll LB 1990. (3-5)
The culture, history and geography of China are explored.

• **Chinese New Year**
by Tricia Brown;
Henry Holt 1987. (3-5)
A description of this centuries-old spring holiday that families celebrate in different ways.

• **Early China**
by Denise Goff;
Trafalgar Square 1986. (3-5)
An account of the history of China, highlighting the Han dynasty and religious beliefs, plus developments in industry and science.

• **The Ancient Chinese**
by Hazel M. Martell;
MacMillan 1993. (4-6)
A history of early China with emphasis on culture and accomplishments.

• **China**
by Peggy Ferroa;
Marshall Cavendish 1991. (4-7)
Unusual facts highlight this look at China, with emphasis on culture.

• **The Moon Lady**
by Amy Tan;
MacMillan 1992. (4-6)
A grandmother in the United States remembers her childhood in China.

• **City Kids in China**
by Peggy Thomson;
Harper LB 1991. (4-7)
A look at the lives of children in a "typical" Chinese city.

• **Sweet and Sour: Tales from China**
by Carol Kendall and Li Yao-wen;
Houghton 1979 (5-7)
A collection of Chinese folktales.

• **Young Fu of the Upper Yangtze**
by Elizabeth Foreman Lewis;
Henry Holt 1973. (5-8)
Young Fu must pay back a debt of $5 or face public shame. Newbery Medal winner for 1933.

• **Science in Ancient China**
by George Beshore;
Watts LB 1988. (5-7)
An introduction to scientific achievements, such as gunpowder, in ancient China.

• **The Terra Cotta Army of Emperor Qin**
by Caroline Lazo;
MacMillan 1993. (5-8)
The story of the 7,500 terra-cotta figures that guard the tomb of China's first emperor.

Historical Aid

No one knows for sure when people first came to the land now called China but its written history goes back about 3,500 years. The Chinese call their country *Chung-kuo*, which means *Middle Country*. This name may have come into being because the ancient Chinese thought of their country as both the geographical center of the world and the only truly cultured civilization. The name *China* was given to the country by foreigners. It may have come from *Ch'in* which was the name of an early Chinese dynasty. China has the world's oldest living civilization. Its written history goes back about 3,500 years, and its visual arts date from about 4,000 B.C.

In early times the Chinese people were divided into many small states. In 221 B.C. the Ch'in dynasty established an empire with a strong central government. This empire lasted in some form for more than 2,000 years. Important inventions were developed. Great cities were built. Magnificent works of art and literature were created. During the 1800s the Chinese empire began to weaken. In 1911 revolutionaries overthrew the Manchu dynasty and China became a republic the following year. In 1949 the Chinese Communist Party, led by Mao Zedong, set up another government system, The Peoples' Republic of China. Nationalists fled to the island of Taiwan where they reestablished their own government.

China is the most populated country in the world. Most of the Chinese people belong to the Han nationality which has been the largest in China for centuries. The rest of the population consists of about 50 minority groups including Kazakhs, Mongols, Tibetans and Uigurs.

Family life is extremely important in Chinese culture. Before 1949 the ideal was five generations living under one roof. Family relationships have changed through the years. In the past, a father could legally kill his children if they disobeyed him. In some cases, daughters were killed at birth because girls were considered useless. Today, girls

as well as boys are valued and parents no longer expect their children to show unquestioning obedience. Although the ancient imperial system ended in 1912, the People's Republic of China has maintained many of the great traditions and festivals, and still has a strong commitment to art and literature.

TIME LINE

 Chinese history is divided into dynasties. Each dynasty is a period of time when one family was in power.

2200 B.C.	1700 B.C.	1027 B.C.	221 B.C.
HSIA (XIA)	**SHANG**	**ZHOU (CHOU)**	**CH'IN**
• Dynasty of China is founded. • Potter's wheel is introduced. • Farming begins.	• Horse-drawn chariots are used. • Bronze weapons are cast. Silk is made. • Carving done in jade and ivory. • Historical records carved on tortoise shells.	• Multiplication tables developed. • Casting of bronze and iron containers. • Confucius introduces his theories.	• Chopsticks are invented. • Great Wall is built. • Writing brush is used. • Weights and measures are standardized. • First emperor burns all books.
206 B.C.	220 A.D.	581 A.D.	618 A.D.
HAN	**THREE KINGDOMS**	**SUI**	**T'ANG**
• Confucianism becomes state religion. • Foot stirrups, paper, wheelbarrow and the seismograph are invented. • The Silk Road opens for trade with Asia.	• China is divided into three kingdoms held by the kings of Wei, Shu and Wu. • Buddhism increasingly influences the country.	• China is reunified during this short 37 year-long dynasty.	• Woodblock printing begins. • Multicolor ceramics are produced. • Highly cultural era. Poetry and education flourish.
960 A.D.	1271 A.D.	1368 A.D.	1644 A.D.
SUNG	**YUAN**	**MING**	**CH'ING**
• Magnetic compass invented. • Gunpowder used in fireworks. • Landscape paintings are produced.	• Foreign travel is banned. • Great Wall is restored. • Marco Polo of Venice visits and takes news of China back to the world.	• Blue and white porcelain is produced. • Art and literature flourish.	• China expands to Tibet, Mongolia & Central China. • Red and green pottery glazes developed. • Peking Opera established.

 In 1912 the Republic of China—Dr. Sun Yat-sen gains control of China and attempts to unite the country. Communist power increases through the years. **Important names to remember:** Chiang Kai-shek, Mao Zedong

GEOGRAPHY

Historical Aid

what are the 2 largest

China is the third largest country in the world in area. Its vast land area includes some of the world's driest deserts (Gobi), highest mountains (Mt. Everest), longest rivers (Yangtze) and most populated cities (Shanghai). China can be divided into eight major land regions, including the Tibetan Highlands and the Mongolian Uplands. While most of China's minority peoples live in the border regions and far western parts of the country, these numbers account for only about 5% of the population. Most live in rural villages and small towns, with the remainder living in crowded cities.

Project

Create a map of China that shows some of its geographic regions, cities, landmarks and features.

Materials

- Reference books
- Transparency film
- Construction paper
- Scissors
- Map, following page
- Overhead projector
- Crayons
- Glue

Directions

1. Reproduce the map of China, following, for each student. Make a transparency of the map below to display on an overhead projector.

2. Using the transparency as a guide, have students duplicate the map, coloring each region and feature. Use reference books to have students add at least two additional geographical details to individual maps. Cut out maps and mount on construction paper for display. Have a sharing session in which students tell a little about their additions.

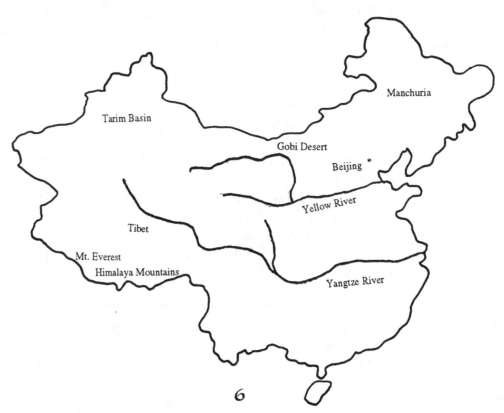

Historical Aid

Chinese, the oldest written language in the world, is made up of *ideographs*, pictures of ideas rather than letters of the alphabet. Each ideograph, or character, is a symbol that represents a complete word or syllable. Chinese written language, added to over the years, now consists of as many as 50,000 symbols. A person who knows about 6,500 of the most frequently used characters can read a Chinese newspaper or modern novel.

Characters have changed from ancient to modern times. A simple ideograph consists of only one character. There are 11 basic strokes that are written in proper sequence. The simplest word has one stroke, the most complicated has 30.

Project

Create a decorative border for the classroom using a combination of existing Chinese and student-created ideographs.

Materials

- Paper
- Pencil
- Scratch paper
- Paint brushes
- Ideograph character page, following
- Half-sheets white construction paper
- Red and black tempera paint
- Masking tape

Directions

1. Reproduce the ideograph character page or display it where everyone can see it.

2. Practice writing the ideographs on scratch paper. Create several original ideographs as well.

3. Choose two ideographs to recreate with paint. One should be from the character page, the other should be an original.

4. Paint each symbol with red or black paint on the construction paper. Write the translation in paint underneath the character.

5. Create a decorative border on the classroom wall by taping the painted characters side by side. Use them as a reference for other Chinese writing activities.

sun

moon

vehicle

horse

man

heart

tree

eyes

fish

mouth

dog

hand

go

field

see

stream

return

father

make

walk

Historical Aid

Chinese pictures dating back 3,500 years have been found scratched onto the surface of animal bones and tortoise shells. These inscriptions, called *oracle bones,* were used by diviners, people who try to tell the future, to answer questions put to them by the king. Some questions were about ordinary topics like how to cure a toothache or when to hunt. Others asked how to win on the battlefield.

After the inscriptions were scratched, the diviner drilled shallow pits into the surface on the reverse and put a heated rod into each pit. The cracks that appeared were understood to mean either "yes" or "no".

The Chinese writing characters used today developed from these early pictures.

Project

Create a replica of an oracle bone.

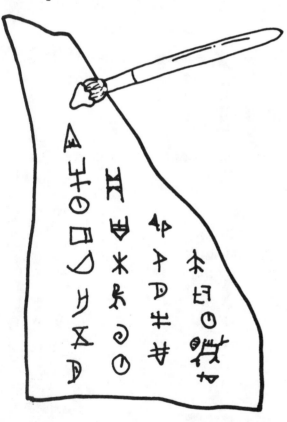

Materials

• Brown paper bag

• Starch

• Wide-bristle paint brush

• Scissors

• Light-colored crayons (white, pink, yellow)

• Watercolor paints and brush

Directions

1. Cut open the paper bag and lay flat. Cut a large, irregular shape from the bag.

2. "Paint" the irregular shape with starch and allow to dry and stiffen overnight.

3. Use the crayon to write picture symbols on the stiffened bag.

4. Brush the entire bag shape with a brown watercolor wash to make the symbols appear scratched on the surface.

WOOD WRITING

Historical Aid

Before the Chinese invented paper in 105 A.D., they recorded events and stories by writing characters from top to bottom on wooden strips. When the strip was full, its surface would be cut off with a knife so the clean surface below could be written on.

When writing was completed on a number of strips, the strips were placed sequentially, tied together with string and rolled into a "book". The title was written on the front of the book.

Project

Make a rolled wooden strip book that tells a story in both ancient Chinese format and modern English format.

Materials

- Fine-tipped marking pens
- Wooden craft or popsicle sticks (8 per project)
- Scissors
- String
- Clean, empty coffee (or other wide-mouth) cans

Directions

1. Review the ideograph meanings (page 9) and the ideograph border created by the class (page 8).

2. With marking pen, use ideographs to write a short story on the eight sticks. Remember to write from top to bottom on each stick and to place them in sequential order from left to right.

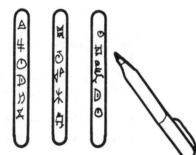

3. When the story is complete, tie the craft sticks together by following the steps illustrated at right.

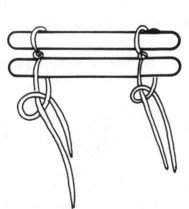

4. Turn the "book" over and write a simple translation for the story across the sticks in current writing patterns, left to right.

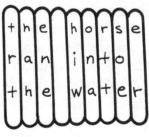

5. Roll the craft sticks closed. Put them upright in cans and place the cans in the classroom library. Invite students to read the ancient "books". Can they interpret the ideographs? Turn the "book" over and read the translation to find out.

SILK

Historical Aid

According to Chinese legend, silk was discovered about 2700 B.C. when Emperor Huang-Ti ordered his wife to find out what was damaging his mulberry trees. She found worms eating the leaves and when she dropped a cocoon into hot water, a slender thread unwound. Silk became so valuable that the punishment for revealing the method of silk-making to a foreigner was punishable by death. The Chinese guarded their methods for about 3,000 years.

Silk had many uses. Rich men and women in ancient China wore long silk robes held in place at the waist. Boots and shoes were also made of silk. Important documents were written on silk scrolls. Banners and flags were made from silk. Bolts of silk were valuable commodities for trading as well.

Project

Create a picture chart that shows the sequential steps in silk-making.

Materials

• Sequential picture page, following, reproduced for each student
• White drawing paper
• Crayons
• Scissors
• Glue

Directions

1. Color the pictures and cut them apart.

2. Glue the steps in silk making to the top of the plain white paper. Read the steps. Match the pictures to the steps and arrange them in sequential order. Glue the pictures in order on the other half of the drawing paper to create a picture chart that illustrates the steps in silk-making.

Step 1
The leaves are picked from the mulberry trees that have been cultivated by the men of the family.

Step 2
The silkworms are stored in bamboo trays on shelves and fed as many mulberry leaves as they can eat.

Step 3
The silkworm spins a cocoon.

Step 4
The cocoon is dropped into boiling water so the silk fiber can be unwound.

Step 5
The thread is plucked from the hot water with chopsticks.

Step 6
The thread is twisted into strands on a spinning machine.

Step 7
Silk strands are woven together on a hand loom.

Step 8
The woven silk is dyed and hung to dry.

Step 1

The leaves are picked from the mulberry trees that have been cultivated by the men of the family.

Step 2

The silkworms are stored in bamboo trays on shelves and fed as many mulberry leaves as they can eat.

Step 3

The silkworm spins a cocoon.

Step 4

The cocoon is dropped into boiling water so the silk fiber can be unwound.

Step 5

The thread is plucked from the hot water with chopsticks.

Step 6

The thread is twisted into strands on a spinning machine.

Step 7

Silk strands are woven together on a hand loom.

Step 8

The woven silk is dyed and hung to dry.

SCROLLS

Historical Aid

Many works by Chinese painters were done on silk scrolls or banners that could be rolled for storage and safekeeping. Some scrolls showed scenes from everyday life. Others, used at the head of funeral processions, showed scenes from Chinese legends depicting the journey people believed took place after death.

Artists of the Yuan period often combined fine writing, called *calligraphy,* with paintings of bamboo. The brush consisted of a wooden or bamboo handle with bristles of animal hair arranged to form an extremely fine point. They usually painted with black ink made of pine soot and glue. Vegetable or mineral pigments were sometimes added to the ink for color.

Project

Paint a Chinese scroll that features bamboo.

Materials

- Long, narrow piece of white butcher paper
- Paint brush
- Black tempera paint, diluted slightly
- Scratch paper
- Thin ribbon
- Paper towels

Directions

1. Demonstrate the method for painting bamboo:

- *Dip the brush bristles in the diluted paint.*
- *Gently press the tips of the bristles together.*
- *Lay the length of the bristles on the paper.*
- *Turn the brush slightly before lifting it off the paper.*
- *Connect the leaves with wide vertical lines.*

2. Practice the technique on scratch paper. When the technique is comfortably mastered, paint the butcher paper.

3. Display the scrolls on the classroom wall for a while. When it's time to transport them home, roll each and tie with a thin ribbon.

WALL POSTERS

Historical Aid

Big-character wall posters served as a means of communication and personal expression in China for many years. People used the posters to express their opinions. They hung them on walls in parks and other public areas. In the late 1970s many people began using posters to complain about the political system. In 1980 the Chinese government outlawed the practice of hanging posters.

Communication in China comes under strict government control. Hundreds of government-published newspapers and handwritten news sheets are printed daily.

Project

Make a big-character wall poster that expresses one or more personal opinions.

Materials

- Butcher paper cut into poster size
- Marking pens
- Crayons
- Masking tape

Directions

1. Discuss the meaning of *opinion*. Share examples and invite students to do the same.

2. Students choose one or more opinions to express in poster form. Write the opinion(s) in large letters that can be seen from a distance.

3. Decorate the poster's edges with Chinese designs.

4. Hang on the classroom wall. Use the opinions expressed on the posters as springboards to classroom discussion and debate. Discuss the phrase "freedom of expression".

HAND COUNTING

Historical Aid

The Chinese often go to an outdoor marketplace to purchase the food and goods they need. The marketplace is a busy, noisy hub of activity. The Chinese have a way of indicating the numbers 1 to 10 with the fingers on one hand. This is very useful where signing may be more effective than shouting the number of items one wants to buy.

Project

Learn to count to ten in the Chinese manner by using the fingers on one hand.

Materials

• Hand

• Paper

• Pencil

Directions

1. Reproduce a copy of the ten hand positions for each child. Together, practice putting the fingers into the correct positions.

2. Provide each student with paper and pencil and challenge students to record ten numbers presented with Chinese hand counting. Present simple math problems in the same way and invite students to record the answer.

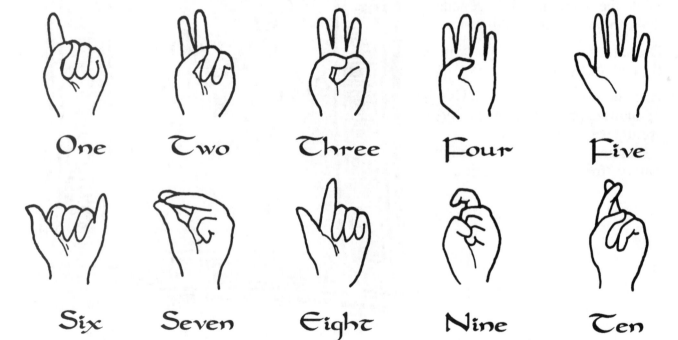

One	Two	Three	Four	Five
Six	Seven	Eight	Nine	Ten

YIN YANG

Historical Aid

Ancient Chinese believed that many spirits lived in mountains, streams and trees, in the air, wind, thunder and rain. But apart from believing they had to worship spirits and gods, they also thought the universe depended on the balance of two forces—*Yin* and *Yang*. Each force stood for things that were equal but opposite. *Yin* meant dark, weak, female, night, moon and Earth. *Yang* meant bright, strong, male, day, sun and Heaven. If these forces did not balance, evils such as droughts or floods might occur.

The Chinese tried to achieve this balance by carefully choosing sites for buildings and burial grounds. Imbalance in the body was healed with herbs and foods.

Project

Make a paper project that shows the balance of the forces of *Yin* and *Yang*.

Materials

• Two 12-inch (31 cm) construction paper circles, one black and one white

• Glue

• Scissors

• Black marking pen

Directions

1. Cut the white construction paper as shown in the diagram (1).

2. Place the white shape on top of the black as shown in diagram (2).

3. Glue in place.

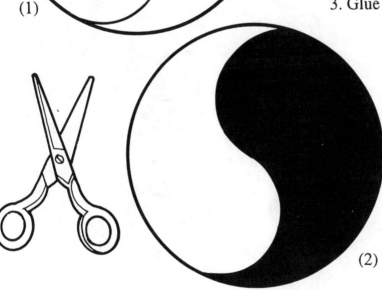

(1)

(2)

ZODIAC

Historical Aid

The Chinese zodiac moves in a cycle of 12 years, each named for an animal. Legend has it that Buddha once summoned all the animals of the kingdom to his bedside. Only 12 came and, in order of their appearance, he dedicated a year to each. The rat was the first, followed by the ox, tiger, hare, dragon, snake, horse, sheep, monkey, rooster, dog and pig.

The people born during the year of a particular animal are said to possess certain characteristics. Review the chart on the Zodiac Comparison page, following, to find out what years and characteristics are represented by each animal in the zodiac.

Project

- Create a paper project that depicts the 12 animals in the Chinese zodiac.
- Use the Zodiac Comparison page to make a personalized characteristic comparison. Draw conclusions as to the chart's validity.

Directions

1. Color and cut out the animal patterns.

2. Glue the animals to the outer edge of the paper circle. Begin with the rat in the 12:00 position and continue clockwise with the animals in the order shown in the illustration.

3. Decorate the center of the paper circle with oriental designs.

Materials

- Construction paper circle, 12 inches (30 cm) in diameter
- Scissors
- Glue
- Crayons
- Animal patterns, following page, reproduced for each student
- Zodiac Comparison page (page 20)

Zodiac Comparison

Year 1: *Year of the Rat* — 1972, 1984 — Charming, bright, creative, thrifty
Year 2: *Year of the Ox* —1973, 1985 — Steadfast, methodical, dependable
Year 3: *Year of the Tiger* —1974, 1986 — Dynamic, warm, sincere, a leader
Year 4: *Year of the Hare* — 1975, 1987 — Humble, artistic, clearsighted
Year 5: *Year of the Dragon* —1976, 1988 — Flamboyant, imaginative, lucky
Year 6: *Year of the Snake* —1977, 1989 — Discreet, refined, intelligent
Year 7: *Year of the Horse* — 1978, 1990 — Sociable, competitive, stubborn
Year 8: *Year of the Sheep* —1979, 1991 — Artistic, fastidious, indecisive
Year 9: *Year of the Monkey* —1980, 1992 — Witty, popular, versatile, good-humored
Year 10: *Year of the Rooster* —1981, 1993 — Aggressive, alert, perfectionist
Year 11: *Year of the Dog* —1982, 1994 — Honest, conservative, sympathetic
Year 12: *Year of the Pig* —1983, 1995 — Caring, industrious, home-loving

Choose four classmates. List their name and birth year. Find their animal sign and write it in the correct column. Compare their personality traits to those of their sign. Draw one or two conclusions about the similarities or differences. Write the conclusions in the column.

Person	Birth Year Animal Sign	Conclusions
1.		
2.		
3.		
4.		

Historical Aid

Many of today's familiar toys such as kites, frisbees, yo-yos and jump ropes had their origins in China. Ancient Chinese played board games that continue to be played today. *Weiqi*, or "Go", around for thousands of years, is one of the most complicated board games in the world because of the high number of possible moves. Mah-jongg, similar to many card games but played with tiles engraved with Chinese drawings, has been played since 500 B.C.

Sporting events are a favorite pastime in modern China. Popular sports in the country include basketball, table tennis and volleyball.

Project

Plan and participate in a "Chinese play day" that includes a variety of outdoor recreation and indoor games.

Materials

• Recreation Suggestion Page, following

• Sporting equipment and games, as determined by students

Directions

1. Involve students in planning the play day. Reproduce several copies of the Recreation Suggestion page to distribute among them. Discuss the options, make selections, then create a "master schedule". Write it on the butcher paper. Display the schedule.

2. Divide into cooperative groups to assign responsibility for gathering the materials and equipment and setting up the various activities.

Outdoor Games

Kite Flying: Kite flying was a Chinese invention of the 3rd century B.C. You can make kites as a class project (see page 23) or purchase inexpensive ones from the store.

Frisbee Throwing: A favorite ancient Chinese game was disk-throwing similar to the plastic frisbees of today. Plan a group frisbee toss or a distance contest.

Badminton: Ancient Chinese children played a game similar to badminton. Provide a net, rackets and shuttlecocks.

Chinese Jump Rope: A Chinese jump rope is similar to a large, sturdy rubber band. Two players stand opposite each other and stretch the band around their ankles while others take turns jumping in and out and making patterns with the rope. The rope starts at the ankles and is raised higher and higher with each turn.

Basketball, Volleyball: Divide into teams for a fun-filled game.

Indoor Games

Leaf Game: Many Chinese games make use of natural materials. Several players may play this game. One player puts a leaf in the center of a table. Other players try to flip the leaf over by slapping their own leaf down near it. If the air current produced succeeds in doing that, they get to keep the leaf in the center. Players take turns putting a leaf in the center.

Jacks: The original game was played with knucklebones of small animals! Learn to play with the modern metal variety.

Yo-yos: This hand-held toy originated in China. Learn how to use a yo-yo. Those who know advanced moves may teach classmates.

Table Tennis: Scale this game down to an indoor version. Obtain a standard net to suspend across a classroom table. Use a standard ball, as well, but use hands as paddles.

Gymnastics: Spread a throw rug or mat on the floor and practice simple gymnastic moves.

Board Games: Wealthy adults in ancient China played a game similar to Backgammon. You may also look for the games "Go" or "Mah-jongg" in a toy store.

KITES

Historical Aid

The Chinese claim that one of their generals, Han Sin, invented the kite in 206 B.C. for use in war. As kites became used for recreation they became a form of artistic expression. Lanterns, insects, storks, flowerpots and people are but some of the unusual shapes. Some kites have clappers and gongs which create music when flown. All are elaborately decorated. Those with lunar designs are used in festivals.

The ninth day of the ninth month is set aside as Kites' Day. A legend tells that hundreds of years ago a man dreamed that misfortune would strike his household. He took his family and flew kites for the day. Upon return, they found their home in ruins. The thousands of kites flown on Kites' Day celebrate this event and are supposed to float away evil spirits.

Project

Construct an unusually shaped and decorated Chinese kite.

Materials

• Tissue paper in various colors

• Cardboard cut in thin strips

• Scissors   • String   • Marking pens

Directions

1. Provide some basic guidelines for creating the kite:

   • Children may work alone or cooperatively.

   • Create a frame using cardboard strips and strings. Bend the strips and tie them with string to create the desired shape.

   • Be sure the cardboard crosses in the center so that string can be attached for flying.

   • Decorate the tissue paper with marking pens **after** the kite is completed. Don't overdo it!

2. Brainstorm a list of possible kite shapes.

3. Provide the materials. Encourage experimentation with different shapes and tissue paper arrangement. Their kite may not fly but remember: Chinese kites are also an art form!

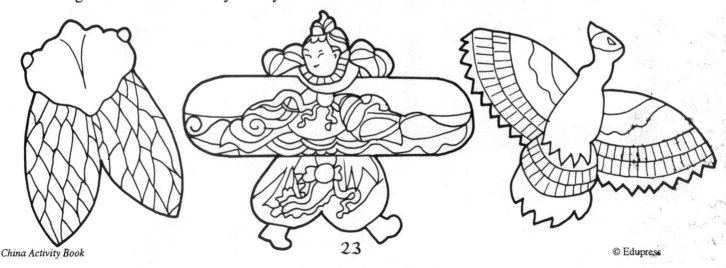

LITERATURE

Historical Aid

Chinese literary works, some of the world's oldest, date back 3,000 years. Writing was graceful regardless of the topic. Many masterpieces of Chinese literature deal with subjects such as history, philosophy, politics, religion and science. They often teach a moral lesson or express a political philosophy. These themes appear especially in the writings of Confucius, who lived from about 551 to 479 B.C.

Traditional Chinese poetry was closely associated with painting. One famous poet, Wang Wei, wrote four-line poems that delicately describe scenes from nature.

Project

Write a four-line poem describing a scene or subject from nature. Paint a picture to illustrate the poem.

Materials

- Writing paper
- Pencil
- Watercolor paints and brushes
- Painting paper
- Various colors construction paper
- Glue or tape for mounting

See the graceful bird.
It flies to its nest.
There it doesn't say a word.
It really likes to rest.

Directions

1. Begin by brainstorming some scenes or subjects from nature. Compile the list on the chalkboard.

2. Each child should select a subject or scene from the list and write a four-line poem about it.

3. Paint a picture to illustrate the poem. Mount both to a backing of coordinating construction paper for display.

TOMB FURNITURE

Historical Aid

During the Shang dynasty ritual funerals were held for kings in which all their worldly possessions—jade, bronze weapons, ivory, pottery, mystical instruments—were buried along with human and animal sacrifices. Sometimes hundreds of people and entire zoos were killed. The Shang made magnificent bronze objects decorated with mythical beasts and formal patterns to bury in the main part of the tomb, a deep pit, dug 30 to 40 feet (9.14 to 12.19 m) into the ground. The entrances were sometimes guarded by dead sentries armed with bronze weapons.

The practice of human and animal sacrifice ended with the Shang dynasty. From the Han period on, clay figures replaced people and animals. Han tombs were also richly furnished, and the walls covered with carved stones, pottery tiles or paintings showing happy scenes, dances, musical entertainments, meals and processions.

Project

Make a collage that shows the worldly possessions that would be buried in your tomb if you lived during the Shang dynasty.

Materials

- Construction paper
- Magazines and catalogs
- Photographs (student supplied)
- Scissors
- Glue
- Paper
- Pencil

Directions

1. Make an inventory list of all worldly possessions including family members and pets.

2. Use the inventory list as a checklist for gathering pictures—actual photographs, original drawings or magazine pictures—of all possessions.

3. Arrange the possessions in a collage on construction paper. Glue in place.

Historical Aid

Ancient wealthy Chinese wore skirts and robes made of silk, dyed and embroidered with designs. Flat-heeled shoes and gloves of silk adorned feet and hands. Men wore hats, women went bare-headed but fashioned their hair in elaborate styles held in place with long pins and jewelry. Field workers and farmers wore short tunics tied at the waist with trousers that came just below the knee.

An emperor's robes were highly decorative and had ceremonial significance. On the longest night of the year a blue robe was worn. On the longest day the robe was yellow. One of 12 dragon symbols was commonly embroidered on the robe to denote power, knowledge, fertility and well-being.

Project

Make a cooperative mural that resembles the dragon robe worn by an emperor.

Materials

- Yellow and blue butcher paper
- Tempera paint
- Paint brushes
- Cloth or crepe paper strip the width of the robe

Directions

1. Cut two or more emperor's robes from butcher paper. (See illustration.)

2. Divide into cooperative groups of 4-6 students per robe.

3. Sketch one or several dragons on the robe. Paint the dragon and allow the paint to dry.

4. Surround the dragon with swirls and of bright paint in various colors.

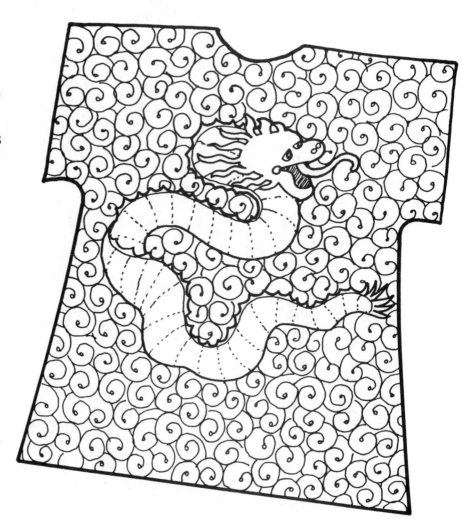

Historical Aid

Perhaps the greatest Chinese invention of all was paper. Printing surfaces were already being made from silk fibers but this method was expensive. An experiment in 105 A.D. with rags and plants mashed with water evolved into pressed sheets of paper. By 700 A.D. printing techniques had advanced to wooden blocks.

Many Chinese inventions came from everyday experiences. Examples include the wheelbarrow, horse collar, odometer, waterwheel, umbrella, eyeglasses, mechanical clock, paper money, earthquake detector and kites. Others such as the compass and gunpowder may well have changed history.

Project

Review the invention-related projects and choose one or several to complete.

Materials

• Provide materials needed for each project as listed on the Invention Project page, following.

Directions

1. Photocopy several copies of the invention information page.

2. Divide into cooperative groups of three or more and give each group the opportunity to select a project to complete.

3. Set a time limit for completion, then provide time for each group to share its projects and present its findings.

Compass

The maritime compass was first used over 2,000 years ago when the Chinese discovered that magnetite would point to a north-south direction automatically. This enabled long-distance sea travel.

Give several examples of instances where a compass is used. Take classmates on a short hike in which the compass is used and directions are called out as the hike progresses.

Wheelbarrow

Toiling in the fields meant moving materials and tools to different places. In order to make better use of time, a wheeled cart was invented.

Demonstrate a wheelbarrow's advantages in a race. Gather two piles of ten identical things. Some should be small, some large. At a signal, one person using just his or her hands and one using a wheelbarrow move their piles to a finish line.

Umbrella

Some simple Chinese inventions have proven through time to make life easier and more enjoyable. Some examples are paper, umbrella, eyeglasses, mechanical clock, odometer and kite.

Present an oral demonstration that shows the benefits of the Chinese inventions listed above. Use actual examples that show life with and without these inventions.

Earthquake Detector

The many earthquakes that struck China made it necessary to create a way to detect them. This was achieved in 132 A.D. with a bronze vase made of eight carved dragons, each with a ball in its mouth. The balls fell when the earth trembled!

Find out how earthquakes are detected and recorded now. Use pencil and paper to demonstrate how a seismograph works.

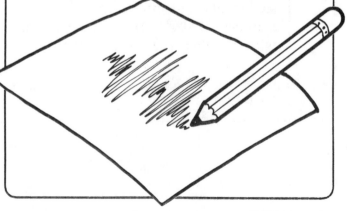

TRANSPORTATION

Historical Aid

During the Han and T'ang dynasties wealthy families traveled in sedan chairs carried by two men. For the poor, the most useful vehicle was a wooden wheelbarrow. People of modern China are carrying loads in the same way their ancestors would have 2,000 years ago. Wooden carts serve as load haulers. Large barges still carry heavy cargo along the rivers. While railroads have been built and some roads have been paved, most people still travel by bicycle or on foot. The rugged terrain in China has always made the building of roads and improvement of transportation difficult.

Project

Play some games based on the different modes of transportation in ancient and modern China.

Materials

- Two wheelbarrows
- Two buckets
- Paperback books
- Two large stuffed animals
- Paper
- Two chairs with arms
- Four 36-inch (one meter) wooden dowels

Directions

1. Gather the equipment and materials needed for the transportation games on this and the following page.

2. Explain the games and safety rules to the students.

3. Divide into smaller groups, if desired, and rotate the groups from one game to the next until they have participated in all. Adult supervision will be needed at each game station.

 Courier

In ancient China, message couriers traveled from station to station, delivering messages as they went.

Divide into four-member teams. Position the teams in two large rectangles of equal size with a student at each corner. Give one child on each team a folded "letter". At the starting signal, the child with the letter races clockwise to the next person, or courier, in the rectangle. The race continues until all couriers have carried the letter and the last one is back to the starting point.

 ## Load Carrier

People still haul loads by balancing them on sticks carried across their shoulders as they did 2,000 years ago.

Hang a bucket on each end of the dowel. The first team to balance the load by filling each bucket with four or more paperback books is the winner!

 ## Sedan Chairs

The wealthy of ancient China rode in sedan chairs held by long, strong poles. The chair was lifted by male servants and carried to its destination.

Put two dowels through the chair arms. Set a large stuffed animal in the seat. At a signal, two players on opposite sides of the chair lift it by the poles and carry it to a finish line. At that point, the chair is carried back to the start by two other players. Repeat until all team members have a turn. If the passenger (the stuffed animal) tumbles from the seat, the players return to their starting point.

 ## Wheelbarrows

Wooden carts and the invention of the wheelbarrow enabled the Chinese of yesterday and today to stack and haul loads of goods.

The team to fill a wheelbarrow with the highest load (books, jackets, stuffed animals, etc.) and move it 12 feet (4 meters) without anything falling off is the winner.

MARTIAL ARTS

Historical Aid

The Chinese have been practicing some form of exercise for thousands of years. Exercise is an important part of their day, with many workers incorporating exercise as part of their morning rituals. Most exercises stress control, concentration and balance. Even those that incorporate a form of kick boxing stress beauty rather than fighting. Three main types of Chinese exercise are *tai chi chaun*, *Qi gong* and *Wushu*. They are explained further below.

Project

Spend a few moments each morning practicing a form of Chinese exercise.

Materials

• Clock timer
• Paper tubing (for *Wushu*)

Directions

Review the different types of Chinese exercise. Set the timer and do four minutes of one form of exercise. Rotate the exercises daily.

Tai Chi

Tai chi chuan, known as *tai chi*, combines graceful, circular movements with deep breathing. Basic exercises in tai chi have unusual names such as "Grasp the Bird's Tail" and "Wave Hands Like a Cloud". With these names in mind, develop some controlled moves to use in your exercise program.

Wushu

Wushu is a form of exercise-fighting practiced as self defense. Weapons such as sabers, spears, swords and clubs are sometimes used for beauty rather than fighting. One form of *wushu* requires strength while another employs cunning. The latter imitates movements of 12 different birds and animals: dragon, tiger, monkey, horse, snake, eagle, sparrow, turtle, and praying mantis. Use a paper towel tube as a saber to emulate the first form. Imitate animal movements to emulate the second.

Qi gong

Qi gong is a form of deep breathing exercises aimed at achieving longevity by regulating the mind, body and breath. *Qi gong* can be directed to various parts of body to increase strength, decrease pain and control disorders such as high blood pressure. Practice some deep breathing while focusing concentration on a particular body part.

Food

Historical Aid

Grain is the main food in China. Most adults eat more than one pound (.5 kilogram) a day. Rice is the favorite grain among people in the south. In the north, people prefer wheat, which they make into bread and noodles. Everyday meals include *fan*, which is grain and *cai*, meaning any food cut into bite-sized pieces. *Cai* is usually vegetables, perhaps with bits of chicken, pork or seafood. Meat makes up only a small part of the Chinese diet. Unusual foods such as bear paws and camel hooves are eaten as well. Food is usually steamed or stir-fried. Meals are eaten with chopsticks and spoons—knives stay in the kitchen.

Project

Prepare Chinese-style food and recipes to sample or in preparation for a multi-course Chinese banquet, page 34.

Materials

• See individual recipes and snack ideas

❀ *There are thousands of varieties of tea cultivated in China. While boiled water or beer may be taken with the food, meals usually begin and end with the favored beverage—tea.*

Select several teas to brew and sample.

❀ *Chinese cabbage is one of the oldest food crops of China. It has wide, thick leaves which form long cylindrical heads.*

Finely chop Chinese or other variety cabbage. Coat with rice vinegar.

❀ *The Chinese vary their diet with many vegetables especially cucumbers, eggplant, radishes, tomatoes and turnips.*

Select some vegetables to cut into thin slices or flower shapes.

❀ *Many meals revolve around the over 7,000 varieties of rice grown in China.*

Boil or steam rice according to package directions. Season with soy sauce.

❀ *Exploded rice looks and tastes like crispy rice cereal and is eaten as a snack or pressed together with syrup to make a cookie.*

Munch on crispy rice cereal or make crispy rice treats according to package directions.

❀ *Chinese eat* mien, *or noodles, in all shapes and lengths boiled in plain soup or fried. Master noodle makers are very skilled. Long noodles symbolize long life and are served at birthday celebrations.*

Boil water and cook *mien* (noodles) according to package directions. Season with soy sauce. If *mien* is not available, cook pasta.

❀ *Ordinary meals do not include dessert; they often end with soup. Soup may be served as a course during a banquet.*

For 8 servings of *egg flower soup*, mix:
• 2 T (30 ml) cornstarch
• 4 T (30 ml) cold water
until no longer lumpy
• Beat 2 eggs separately
• Boil 6 (152 ml) cups
  canned chicken broth

Add the cornstarch mixture to the soup. Stir soup until thickened. Slowly pour beaten egg into the soup. Egg will form shreds.

❀ **Fu yong** *is a vegetable pancake-type dish popular in southern China.*

Combine
• 4 well-beaten eggs
• ½ lb. (1 kg) fresh
  bean sprouts
• thinly sliced green
  onion
• small can tuna

Mix together and drop by spoonful into heated oil in a large frying pan. Cook each pancake until lightly browned.

❀ *A scarcity of fuel brought about the quick stir-frying method of cooking thinly sliced food in a wok, or bowl-shaped frying pan.*

Cut beef or chicken into thin slices. Stir-fry in a small amount of oil over medium-high heat in a *wok* or deep frying pan.

❀ *Every region has fruit specialties, such as bananas and oranges in the south and apples and peaches in the north.*

Slice bananas, oranges, apples and peaches. Skewer one slice of each on a toothpick.

❀ *The Chinese are poetic about names of dishes. There is usually a story to go along with the recipe.*

Ants Crawling Up a Tree Trunk
Ground meat cooked with
transparent bean vermicelli.
Red-beaked Green Parrots
Spinach served with
boiled bean curd.
Monk Jumps Over the Wall
Dried seafood stewed
in a clay pot.

Make up your own Chinese recipe and give it an unusual name. Create a story to describe how the dish got its name.

BANQUET

Historical Aid

The banquet is an important type of recreation in China. On special occasions, such as family weddings, lavish banquets are often held with as many as twenty courses. The table is set especially for each course. There is a saucer for soy sauce, plate, small bowl, chopsticks, spoon and glasses.

A banquet is not grain-based. It might include roast duck, fried whole fish, stir-fried meat and vegetables and other foods prepared and served in an elegant way. The last dish is soup followed by rice or noodles. An emperor's banquet, however, might consist of 132 courses at one sitting!

Project

Work in cooperative groups to plan and carry out the preparation of a multi-course Chinese banquet, using the preceding recipes and/or those found in Chinese cookbooks.

Materials

- Chinese cookbooks for reference
- Chopsticks—available in bulk at the food market
- Plastic spoons
- Paper bowls and plates of varying size
- Butcher paper
- Cooking utensils and ingredients as determined by recipe selection

Directions

1. Besides planning the menu and preparing dishes, students will also be responsible for setting the banquet table.

2. Divide into groups. Review the recipes on the preceding pages. Determine the number of courses that will be served and the responsibilities for each group. Arrange for adult assistance on banquet day.

3. Make a table covering in advance of the banquet. Cut butcher paper to fit the table tops. Decorate using markers.

4. On the day of the banquet, set up areas where each group will prepare its contribution to the banquet. Appoint table setters and banquet servers. Practice using the chopsticks. Enjoy!

BRONZE COINS

Historical Aid

Early Chinese traded with one another by exchanging products such as pottery, vegetables, fruit, meat, cloth, silk, weapons and grain. Bartering continued until people found it more convenient to use money. During the Ch'in dynasty (221 B.C.) bronze discs with a square hole in the middle were used by everyone in the empire.

The round coins were worth 50 units. The knife shape equalled 500 units. The square hole in the center of each enabled them to be strung together, often in hundreds, to make carrying them easier.

Project

Make replicas of ancient Chinese coins to use in math and bartering activities.

Directions

1. Photocopy and cut out the coin patterns.

2. Trace the patterns onto index cards. Cut out the shapes including the center section. Make at least 15 round and 12 knife coins.

3. Paint both sides of the coins. When dry, string onto lengths of cut yarn.

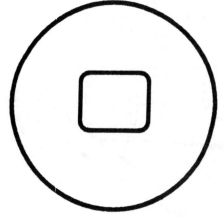

Materials

- Brown and red tempera paint, mixed to create a rusty bronze shade

- Paint brushes
- Scissors
- Yarn or string
- Large index cards
- Pencils
- Coin patterns, below

Activity Suggestions

- Plan a bartering activity. Have children bring old items to sell. They can set their own prices (in multiples of 100), barter for final costs and exchange their coins.
- Use the coins for addition and subtraction problems, counting and place value lessons.

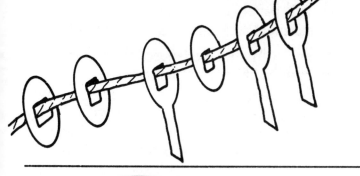

Coin Patterns

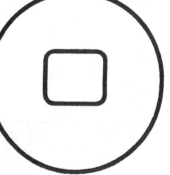

LANDSCAPES

Historical Aid

Painting has been an established art in China since at least the 300s B.C. Painting revolves around subjects such as people, landscapes, flowers, fish, insects, birds and animals. Paintings are done on silk or absorbent paper. A pointed brush applies paint made of mineral and plant pigments. Color is applied in small amounts for a washed look.

During the Sung dynasty, artists painted landscapes called *shan-shui* featuring towering mountains and expanses of water. In these paintings, the artist tried to suggest a harmony between nature and the human spirit.

Project

Create a *shan-shui* landscape painting.

Materials

- Watercolor paints
- Brushes
- Large sheet white construction or painting papers

Directions

1. Discuss the elements of a *shan-shui* painting—towering mountains and water.

2. Provide paper and paint and allow students to interpret these elements in a painting.

3. When dry, mount the landscape paintings on a muted color construction paper.

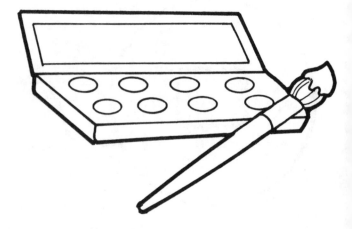

LACQUER WARE

Historical Aid

Lacquer ware is made by applying varnish to such articles as trays, furniture, dishes, vases and boxes. The process was first used during the Han dynasty when lacquer was used to decorate wooden objects and military equipment like shields.

Natural lacquer is obtained from the sap of the lac trees that grow in China. The sap is strained and dried by heat to make a dark brown liquid as thick as syrup. The liquid is diluted and sometimes colored. As many as 35 layers are applied to an object, each one drying before the next layer is applied. Lacquer wares are so durable, they show no wear for hundreds of years.

Project

Use a variation of the technique of lacquering to make a decorative box, bowl, plate or tray. Allow a little time to work on the lacquer ware project each day for a period of five to seven days .

Materials

• Gift boxes of assorted sizes

• Heavy-duty paper bowls and plates

• Tempera paint and wide-bristle brushes

• Plain newsprint paper

• Scissors

• White glue slightly diluted with water

• Empty jars or containers with lids

Directions

1. Cut out LOTS of shapes from the plain newsprint. These could be random shapes or Chinese-related shapes such as flowers and dragons.

2. Put some diluted white glue into each of several empty containers. Mix the glue with tempera paint to create different colors. If the glue is too thick to paint with a brush, dilute with a little more water until desired consistency is achieved.

3. Select an item to lacquer. (To make a tray use just the lid or bottom of a box.) Place a paper shape on the item. Paint over it with the glue mixture to adhere it to the surface. One or a combination of colored glue may be used. Cover the surface completely with "lacquered" shapes. Allow to dry for a day or more. Repeat until at least five layers have been applied.

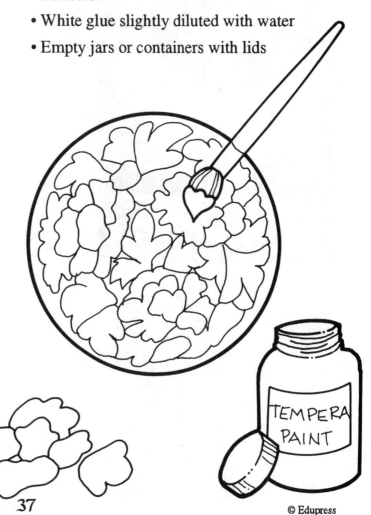

PAPER CUTTING

Historical Aid

The art of paper cutting dates to the T'ang dynasty (618-960 A.D.) Paper cuts are used as decorations and gifts, especially during festive seasons when designs of flowers or symbols of good luck adorn lanterns and houses. Double happiness characters appear during weddings on gifts, candlesticks and incense burners. Paper cuts are also used as stencils for embroidery or prints for clothes and bed linen.

Cut-paper designs may be symmetrical or created as one unbroken piece. They are often handed down from one generation to the next and differ from village to village. Common subjects are birds, animals and opera characters.

Project

Make giftwrap using the art of symmetrical paper cutting.

Materials

• Large rectangle butcher paper, any color

• Various colors plain, lightweight paper

• Scissors

• Glue

Directions

1. Fold the lightweight paper in half.

2. Start at the fold and make one continuous cut in the paper being careful not to cut through the fold again until the cut is complete. Look at the illustrations for ideas.

3. When the cut is complete, unfold the paper and apply a small amount of glue and place the cut paper on the butcher paper. Repeat as often as desired until the butcher paper is covered with paper cuts.

WOODBLOCK PRINT

Historical Aid

Once paper became available, the Chinese invented printing methods. At first, bronze and stone seals were engraved with the names of important people. Ink was applied to the seal and the name could be stamped onto paper. Eventually less costly woodblock printing developed. As a result of this, books could be printed rather than copied by hand.

Creating a woodblock involved several steps. Characters were brushed onto paper and, while wet, were pressed on top of a woodblock covered with rice paper. When the paper was removed a stain remained. An engraving knife was used to cut around the stain. The protruding shapes were brushed with ink. The printer smoothed paper on the inked characters to transfer the print to the paper.

Project

Make a personalized name stamp using the Chinese woodblock printing technique.

Materials

- Styrofoam™ plate or grocery meat tray
- Wide-bristle paint brush
- Glue
- Black tempera paint
- Cardboard
- Lightweight paper
- Scissors

Directions

1. Paint your name in block letters on the paper.

2. Gently press an inverted styrofoam™ plate or tray on the painted name.

3. Lift the plate and allow the paint to dry.

4. Cut around each letter.

5. Cut cardboard large enough to fit the cut letters. Glue the letters in reverse order on the cardboard, also reversing the direction the letters face. (The result will be a mirror image of the name.) Allow the glue to dry.

6. To make a final print, brush the raised letters with paint and press a piece of paper on the painted letters.

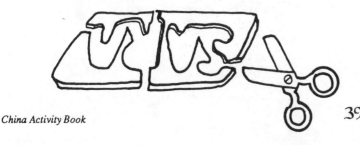

Historical Aid

Jade has always been prized in China as the most valuable of all precious stones, cherished for its beauty and also for its magic. Because it was believed to stop bodies from decaying, a jade *pi*, or disk, was often buried with the dead. The Han emperor Liu Sheng was buried in a suit made of 2,498 pieces of jade that took 10 years to make! During the Han and T'ang dynasties, jade worn as jewelry became a sign of wealth and power.

Jade was difficult to carve because of its hardness. Elaborate processes were developed to carve it into different shapes such as animal figures and delicate vessels. The carvings were so fine that objects often appeared translucent.

Project

Use tissue paper and starch to create a mosaic of a jade object.

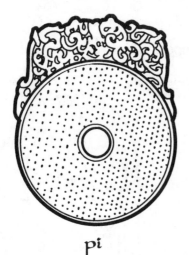

pi

herb vessel

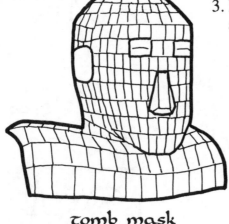

tomb mask

Materials

- Green tissue paper in assorted shades
- Starch (diluted slightly with water)
- Paper cups
- Paper plates
- Paint brushes
- Waxed paper
- Scissors

Directions

1. Cut the tissue paper into small squares.

2. Cut waxed paper into a shape—vase, *pi* disk, mask, animal figure, urn.

3. Pour starch into cups and dilute slightly with water.

4. Lay overlapping pieces of tissue to cover the paper shape, lightly painting each piece as it is positioned with starch mixture.

5. Allow the starch to dry thoroughly. Trim the edges of the paper shape.

EMBROIDERY

Historical Aid

Embroidery is a craft with a long history in China. This type of stitchery was first used with the discovery of silk thread. Pillowcases, blankets, tablecloths, banners, altar cloths, clothes, fans, purses, shoes and pictures are among the objects that are embroidered with traditional motifs such as birds, flowers, cats and goldfish. Flowers, butterflies and geometric designs decorate women's clothes while dragons and bold solid designs decorate men's. Elaborate pieces can take years. They are often worked on by several people.

In early China, a girl's embroidery skill would indicate whether she would make a good wife or not.

Project

Use the technique of embroidery to create a design on fabric.

Materials

- Blunt plastic or other stitchery needles
- Various colors embroidery floss
- Scissors
- Fabric squares
- Embroidery stitch samples

Directions

1. Divide into small groups. Assign each an adult volunteer.

2. Work with each student to teach them how to make a simple embroidery stitch. Recreate the samples below on the chalkboard.

3. Once a simple stitch is mastered, students may complete the embroidery stitch pattern on their fabric square.

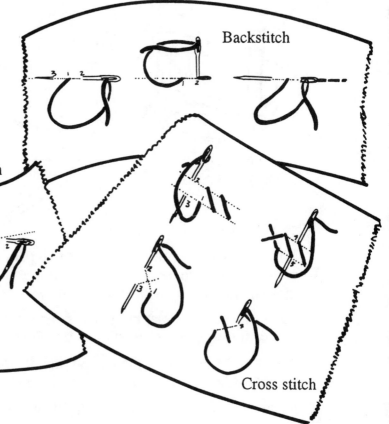

Backstitch

Stem stitch

Cross stitch

HERBS

Historical Aid

Early Chinese discovered that combinations of certain herbs relieved ailments. The T'ang Book of Drugs and Herbs was written during the T'ang dynasty. This information served as the basis for one of the most respected and widely used Chinese books on the subject today. Then and now, brews of herbs, leaves, bark and berries are cooked for hours before being drunk from bowls. More exotic items such as animal horns, dried snakes, lizards and fat glands from the Manchurian frog are added for a stronger brew. Mint is used for relieving headaches. Scrapings of rhinoceros horns cool a fever and tiger bone wine cures aches and pains.

The Chinese pharmacy consists of a large hall with counters on all sides behind which are drawers, each holding an herb. Prescriptions are made by combining the different herbs.

Project

Simulate a Chinese pharmacy in the classroom. Brew peppermint tea to sample.

Materials

Pharmacy

- Resource books about medicinal herbs and Chinese medicine

- Shoe boxes
- Small pads of paper
- Marking pens
- Small plastic bags

Tea
- Peppermint tea
- Cups
- Tea pot
- Hot plate
- Water

Directions

1. To simulate the pharmacy, arrange two parallel tables. Stack one with shoe boxes labeled with names of herbs found during a research session. Add some unusual ingredients, as well, using those mentioned in the historical aid.

2. Fill each box with imaginary herbs. Twigs, leaves, pebbles and aquarium rocks are possible suggestions for use as "mock" herbs. The children can suggest other imaginative substitutions.

3. Take turns role playing the patient, the doctor who writes the prescription (combination of herbs) on the pad of paper, and the pharmacist who fills the prescriptions.

4. At the close of the simulation activity, brew some peppermint tea to enjoy together.

PORCELAIN

Historical Aid

The Chinese made the first real porcelain during the T'ang dynasty. Ming potters improved the methods. But it was the Sung dynasty potters who produced the most elegant porcelain forms in lovely shades of green, blue, gray and ivory to export to the West.

Chinaware differs from other pottery because of its whiteness. The decoration, or *underglaze,* on the porcelain may be applied before the piece is coated with a glaze. The most reliable color is blue made from cobalt and seen in the earliest examples of Chinese porcelain. The secret of making "chinaware" remained with the Chinese until the eighteenth century when German potters finally figured it out.

Project

Paint a porcelain vase in the colors predominantly used in the earliest examples of Chinaware.

Materials

- Blue and white construction paper
- Blue watercolor paint and brushes
- Scissors
- Glue

Directions

1. Cut a vase shape from the white construction paper. Glue the vase to the blue construction paper backing.

2. Paint a design using blue watercolor paints or diluted tempera paint.

China Activity Book

43

© Edupress

FESTIVALS

Historical Aid

In the past, China's people held a number of festivals to celebrate holidays throughout the year. The Communist leaders of China have done away with some of China's traditional festivals and changed others to fit in more closely with their ideas. But festivals are still an important part of life in China.

Some festivals honor ancestors, others an historic event. May Day, which honors working people, and Army Day, honoring the military forces of China, are political in focus. China also observes newer holidays such as National Day, marking the foundation of the People's Republic of China. All are celebrated with parades, demonstrations and other traditional activities.

Project

Plan a day of activities to learn about Chinese festivals and holidays.

Materials

• See individual festivals on this and the following page

Directions

1. Set up three centers in the classroom. Stock each with the materials for the three festivals that are described. Ask parent volunteers to help at each center.

2. Divide into three groups. Make a rotational schedule so that each group has time at all three centers. Allow time at the end of the day to share what was learned.

Ching Ming Festival
Sometime in the month of April.

During **Ching Ming**, which means "pure brightness", families worshiped their ancestors by visiting the local cemetery to tidy up the graves. Afterward they would have a picnic. Sometimes offerings would be made to the kitchen god, one of the most important gods worshiped by the Chinese people. They believed he rose to heaven every year to report their good and bad deeds.

Center activity: Make a "good deed" mural.

Materials
• Butcher paper
• Crayons
• Drawing paper
• Glue

Directions
1. Each child draws a picture of a good deed they have done.
2. Glue the picture on the large sheet of butcher paper. Each group visiting the center adds to the mural.

Dragon Boat Festival
The fifth day of the fifth lunar month.

The **Dragon Boat Festival**, also called *Duanwu Jie,* is held to remember a patriotic poet who drowned himself because the state was taken over by a neighboring state. Dragon boat races are held and rice dumplings are eaten.

Center activity: Make a dragon boat.

Materials
- Half-gallon sized milk carton
- Construction paper
- Scissors   • Glue

Directions
1. Cut off one side of the milk carton.
2. Cut and glue construction paper on the remaining sides and bottom of the carton.
3. Create a cut-paper dragon to glue on the spout end of the carton.

Autumn Moon Festival
The fifteenth day of the eighth lunar month.

The **Autumn Moon Festival** marks the time when the moon is fullest and brightest. The night is filled with lights from brightly colored paper lanterns. Moon cakes made of thin pastry filled with sweet mashed lotus seeds are eaten and given as gifts.

The moon cake tradition is based on an historical event. In the fourteenth century, Chinese cooks aided their country against Mongolian conquerors by stuffing secret messages for a plan of attack inside moon cake dough. The moon cakes were widely distributed and the rebellion was a success.

Center activity: Make mock moon cakes similar to fortune cookies. Have fortune cookies available so each person gets one to munch on while making moon cakes!

Materials
- Brown bags
- Marking pens
- Glue • Scissors

Directions
1. Cut bags into 4-inch (10.16-cm) squares.
2. Write a secret message or fortune inside. Fold the square twice diagonally and glue closed.

You will find a new friend today!

3. Each child should make eight to ten moon cakes to hand out during the day.

NEW YEAR

Historical Aid

One of the most important celebrations is the New Year Festival which marks the beginning of the new year in the Chinese lunar calendar and the beginning of spring. Festival dates vary from year to year, but always start on the first day of the first lunar month, usually between late January and late February. At the New Year everyone becomes a year older and counts his or her age by the number of New Years he or she has seen. Celebrations last for two weeks, although most people are back at work by the fourth day. On the 15th day, a lantern festival marks the end of the celebrations. Everything to ensure good fortune is done. When the Communists came to power they renamed the New Year Festival the Spring Festival. They tried to discourage many of the old customs connected with ancestor worship.

Project

Participate in a variety of activities representative of a Chinese New Year celebration.

Materials

• See material lists for individual activities.

Directions

If possible, time the activities to coincide with the dates of the Chinese New Year. Complete one activity a day.

Spring Cleaning

Since the New Year Festival also marks the beginning of spring, the Chinese preparations start with spring cleaning!

It's time to clean those desks, cupboards, closets and centers! Get everyone involved in a thorough cleaning of the classroom.

NEW YEAR CELEBRATION

Surprise Packets

On the first day of the New Year, children kneel and pay their respects to their elders. In return, they receive little red packets with money inside.

Place a penny inside a folded piece of red paper. Tape to close. Award a packet each time a student does something kind, courteous or respectful.

Firecrackers

At midnight on New Year's Eve, firecrackers are set off to scare away the evil spirits and make a clean start to the new year.

Use a variety of bright tempera paints to make swirls, splatters and bursts to create fireworks on a construction paper background.

Good Luck Signs

Red signs, on which lucky sayings are written, are placed on both sides of the entry door.

May Luck Be With You!

Use marking pens to make good luck signs on red construction paper.
Decorate the edges with ideographs.
Tape to classroom walls.

Paper Lanterns

On the 15th day, a lantern festival marks the end of the New Year's celebration.

Materials
- Tissue paper-12 in. x 16 in.(30 cm x 41 cm)
- Watercolor paints and brushes
- String or yarn • Scissors • Clear tape

Directions
1. Decorate the tissue paper with slightly diluted watercolor designs.
2. When the paint dries, accordion-fold the length of the tissue paper. Open and lay flat. Roll the paper and tape the ends together. Refold the tissue paper.
3. Tape a length of string to the each side of the top for hanging.

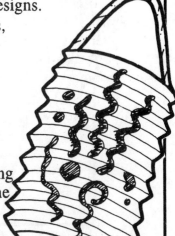

Lion Dance

Bright parades are a common occurrence during New Year celebrations.
Lion dances, accompanied by cymbals, drums and gongs,
are common sights and sounds.

Construct a colorful lion mask to wear in a classroom parade.

Materials
- Paper bags
- Scissors
- Glue
- Beads, sequins and other trims
- Cereal boxes
- Fabric remnants
- Tempera paint
- Yarn
- Fringe
- Paint brushes

Directions
1. Set all materials on a common-use table.
2. Create imaginative lion masks from any or all of the materials provided. Each one should be original and different.
3. Display the colorful lion masks in a parade. Accompany the parade by tapping on aluminum pie tins.